Marks of a True Christian

A Study of Romans 12

By Matthew Allen

© 2024 Spiritbuilding Publishers.
All rights reserved. No part of this book may be reproduced without the publisher's written permission.

Published by
Spiritbuilding Publishers
9700 Ferry Road, Waynesville, OH 45068

MARKS OF A TRUE CHRISTIAN:
A Study of Romans 12
by Matthew Allen

Unless otherwise noted, all Scripture references are taken from the Christian Standard Bible, Copyright 2020 by Holman Bible Publishers. Used by permission. Christian Standard Bible and CSB are federally registered trademarks of Holman Bible Publishers.

ISBN: 978-1-964805-01-6

Spiritbuilding
PUBLISHERS

spiritbuilding.com

Table of Contents

Lesson 1	Living Sacrifices	1
Lesson 2	Don't Be Conformed, Be Transformed	5
Lesson 3	Discerning the Will of God	8
Lesson 4	Do Not Think Too Highly of Yourself	11
Lesson 5	Where Do You Fit?	14
Lesson 6	Genuine Love	17
Lesson 7	Outdo One Another in Sharing Love	20
Lesson 8	Fervent in the Spirit	23
Lesson 9	Rejoice in Hope	27
Lesson 10	Contributing to the Needs of the Saints	30
Lesson 11	Bless Those Who Persecute You	33
Lesson 12	Live in Harmony with One Another	37

Lesson 1

Living Sacrifices

Romans 12:1

Introduction

God has called us to a grand purpose as sons and daughters. We have been called to *shine as lights in the midst of a crooked and twisted generation* (Philippians 2:15). This is accomplished by completely devoting ourselves to God and His calling. Because of His mercy in reaching down to save us, we lead a life of thankfulness.

Thankfulness and purpose are not possible without a deep, abiding relationship with God. How do you approach your spiritual life?

> Therefore, brothers and sisters, in view of the mercies of God, I urge you to present your bodies as a living sacrifice, holy and pleasing to God; this is your true worship (Romans 12:1).

This lesson is intended to accomplish two objectives:

1. We will learn what should motivate us in our service to our Lord.
2. We will learn about what it means to be a living sacrifice.

Remember the Mercies of God

In Romans 12:1a, Paul speaks of the mercies of God. What are God's mercies? Everything. Simply put, *everything we have from God is mercy.* Think of the spiritual reality presented in Romans 1–11. The message is all about God's mercy. He has given us eternal love, grace, peace, joy, strength, hope, and righteousness.

What is your response to God's mercy? *Because he has turned his ear to me, I will call out to him as long as I live,* Psalm 116:2. When we start counting all God has done for us, the call to action in Romans 12:1–2 is the answer.

What generates true devotion is a grasp of salvation's richness.

> Oh, the depth of the riches and the wisdom and the knowledge of God! How unsearchable his judgments and untraceable his

ways! For who has known the mind of the Lord? Or who has been his counselor? And who has ever given to God, that he should be repaid? For from him and through him and to him are all things. To him be the glory forever. Amen (Romans 11:33–36).

This is pure worship. It is an explosion of praise. These are the immeasurable riches given to undeserving sinners. Passages like Ephesians 3:20–21 and Philippians 4:19 should go far in building our confidence *and* devotion. God gives us everything we need according to His infinite riches.

Offer Your Entire Life

In Romans 12:1b, we discover a move from *motivation* to *mandate.* Paul says, *I urge you to present your bodies as a living sacrifice, holy and pleasing to God; this is your true worship.* Let's analyze the language. First, Paul calls on us to **present** ourselves. Using this word would have sparked images of the sacrificial system in the minds of his readers. It refers to temple activity. The Levitical term means "to put it on the altar." In simple terms, it means to die to your agenda. We must die to everything around us—giving all we are as a living and holy sacrifice to God. We hold nothing back.

What do we present? Our **body.** The flesh can dominate. It is the center of desire, depression, and doubts. It must be brought under subjection. Romans 6:12–13 reminds us that it is our responsibility to make sure the body is presented as an instrument of righteousness. Remember, *the body … is for the Lord. The Lord … is for the body,* 1 Corinthians 6:12–13.

Notice how our body is offered as a **living sacrifice**. It is something continually offered or presented. Our humanness wants to take control. We must battle with it. A *living sacrifice is* perpetual, 1 Corinthians 9:27, and must also be offered in living reality. Consider Genesis 22. What did Abraham communicate to God the day he attempted to offer Isaac as a sacrifice? He was saying he would live the rest of his life without anything he held dear—if that was the will of God. Are you prepared to move forward with this type of commitment?

Everything must be offered in humble submission to God. Consider these two passages:

- I have been crucified with Christ, and I no longer live, but Christ lives in me. The life I now live in the body, I live by faith in the Son of God, who

loved me and gave himself for me (Galatians 2:20).
- More than that, I also consider everything to be a loss in view of the surpassing value of knowing Christ Jesus my Lord. Because of him I have suffered the loss of all things and consider them as dung, so that I may gain Christ (Philippians 3:8).

Our offering must be **holy**. Holy means "set apart." Our life must be pure, undefiled, and free from sin. Too many Christians struggle to move into a deeper relationship with God because the body is never brought under the type of subjection God calls for.

Conclusion

Are you moving with thankfulness? With purpose? Let the mercies of God drive you in your motivation to be transformed into a new person. Hold nothing back. Offer your entire self to God. It's the only way you'll effectively wear the *garments of salvation* and *robes of righteousness* you've been clothed with, Isaiah 61:10.

For Discussion

1. What are the mercies of God?

2. Considering how merciful God has been to you, what should be your natural reaction?

3. How do passages like Ephesians 3:20 and Philippians 4:19 fuel your thankfulness? Your confidence?

4. What imagery is connected to the word *present* in Romans 12:1? How does this help you better understand the point of Paul's teaching?

5. What happens to our selfish agenda when we *present* ourselves to God?

6. What does Romans 6:12–13 teach us about our responsibility in getting our body under control?

7. How often do you have to *discipline your body?* See 1 Corinthians 9:27.

8. Is there any part of your old self you're holding back? What is keeping you from sacrificing it for God?

9. To me, to be holy means:

10. I am working to become more holy by:

Lesson 2

Don't Be Conformed, Be Transformed

Romans 12:2a

Introduction

Previously, we discussed how God has called us to a grand purpose, Philippians 2:15. Because of His mercy in reaching down to save us, we lead a life of thankfulness, Colossians 3:15–17. We must develop a deep, abiding relationship with God to accomplish these things. We start the process when we *present (our) bodies as a living sacrifice, holy and acceptable to God*, Romans 12:1.

Today, we move to the next verse in Romans 12. When we "die to our agenda" and hold nothing back, this will come naturally:

> Do not be conformed to this age, but be transformed by the renewing of your mind, so that you may discern what is the good, pleasing, and perfect will of God (Romans 12:2).

In this lesson, we intend to learn how we accomplish the task of being a living sacrifice.

- We will discuss the problem of worldliness.
- We will see the need for transformation.
- We will learn what it means to renew our minds.

Do Not Be Conformed to This World

Worldliness kills any inroads to a deeper relationship with God. Let's look at the negative part of verse 2. Paul says *do not be conformed*. "Conformed" is a word used for "schematic" today. It means "to be stamped like metal" or "to be molded." Here's Paul's imperative: *stop letting yourselves be molded by the world.*

You will never be what God has called you to be if the world's image is stamping you. Do not allow the world to mold you into its kind of thought and behavior.

Write down some troubling worldly trends and behaviors from which the Christian should refrain. Be prepared to share your thoughts.

Be Transformed

This is the positive part of the verse. This transformation should be happening all the time.

Read these passages and comment on how they convey the message of transformation:

    2 Corinthians 3:18:

    Galatians 5:22–25:

    2 Peter 1:5–11:

Renew Your Mind

"Renewal" means to renovate one's thoughts, to alter your thinking completely. This is about the mind, not emotion. The renewed mind is saturated and controlled by the word of God.

Read Psalm 119:11. What is one way you can renovate your mind?

Read Colossians 1:28. What is the purpose of teaching?

Conclusion

Do you spend as much time in the word as you do in the allurements of the world?

Colossians 3:1–3 says:

> So if you have been raised with Christ, seek the things above, where Christ is, seated at the right hand of God. Set your minds on things above, not on earthly things. For you died, and your life is hidden with Christ in God.

How does this passage fit into the overall thought of our lesson?

Lesson 3

Discerning the Will of God
Romans 12:2b

Introduction

Previously, we looked at the beginning of Romans 12:2. What happens when we die to our agenda? We refuse to be programmed or controlled by worldly thinking. The renewing of our minds transforms us. The wording of this part of verse 2 is crucial. Its meaning involves completeness and totality. What was is no more. What is entirely and radically new.

In this lesson, we will move to the next part of verse two in Romans 12. What do transformation and renewal lead to?

> Do not be conformed to this age, but be transformed by the renewing of your mind, **so that you may discern what is the good, pleasing, and perfect will of God** (Romans 12:2).

What are the effects of a renewed mind?

- We will talk about radical reorientation.
- We will talk about how this arms us to choose the will of God.

Radical Reorientation

On what does the *renewed mind* concentrate? Answer: *the will of God.* We must allow God's word to penetrate the deepest recesses of our hearts. The *discerning* in 12:2 is our adoption of the biblical worldview. It involves a giant paradigm shift—a *complete reprogramming of our thinking* **in everything.** As we do, our focus will change, and we will become more and more focused on things of eternal importance. Colossians 3:1–3 fits in well here: *If then you have been raised with Christ, seek the things that are above, where Christ is, seated at the right hand of God. Set your minds on things that are above, not on things that are on earth. For you have died, and your life is hidden with Christ in God.*

For a moment, think about what your mind primarily focuses on each day. If you were to compare spiritual vs. temporal, what would be the most significant percentage of your thoughts?

What are some things you can do to increase the percentage of what is focused on the will of God?

Moral and spiritual growth will result as our worldview shifts from primarily temporal to eternal. When life tests us, our renewed mind will tell us God's will in that situation. This should fill our hearts with hope and confidence.

The Psalmist said: *Your word is a lamp for my feet and a light on my path*. How can we apply this passage to today's lesson? Does this verse fill you with confidence? How?

The Will of God is Good, Acceptable, and Perfect

Notice how God's will is described in the last part of 12:2. God's will is good, acceptable, and perfect. Because of the knowledge gained by the renewed mind, the Christian can choose right over wrong. Spiritual discernment helps us ascertain what God wants us to do. We must then set ourselves to do it.

In daily life, we can each prove God's will and must be concerned about performing God's will.

God's ways work. How can you continue to build your trust in His word?

Conclusion

> For those who live according to the flesh have their minds set on the things of the flesh, but those who live according to the Spirit have their minds set on the things of the Spirit. Now, the mindset of the flesh is death, but the mentality of the Spirit is life and peace.

The attitude of the flesh is hostile to God because it does not submit to God's law. Indeed, it is unable to do so. Those who are in the flesh cannot please God (Romans 8:5–8).

Take a few moments and write down your thoughts on how this passage might be a good summary and conclusion for this lesson.

Lesson 4

Do Not Think Too Highly of Yourself

Romans 12:3

Introduction

These lessons thus far have focused on what is involved in living lives of purpose and thankfulness. We learned from Romans 12:1 that we offer our entire soul, body, mind, and will. This is an essential requirement God lays down for every believer. God wants your life. When you do, God will use you.

Genuinely effective service can only be offered if you offer a living sacrifice. Service to God only has meaning when it is the outflow of total commitment. Total commitment is only total commitment when it produces effective service.

Does a passion for God characterize your spiritual life? A fleshing out of the commitment you've made?

In this lesson, we move to the next verse in Romans 12. What attitude spiritually drives us?

> For by the grace given to me, I tell everyone among you not to think of himself more highly than he should think. Instead, think sensibly, as God has distributed a measure of faith to each one (Romans 12:3).

Most of our Christian life is spent inside the realm of using our spiritual gifts and interacting with others. Romans 12:3 begins the transition into day-to-day expectations for Christians. Notice how we are to think soberly. Before doing anything, we must seek a balanced perception of ourselves. Let's discuss:

- The proper attitude for service.
- Moving forward with faith using the gift(s) God has given you.

The Proper Attitude for Service

What is the basis for the expectation in 12:3? It is given to us by the authority of an apostle. In other words, the verse is authoritative. *Everyone among you...every professed Christian must not think of himself more highly than he ought to think.* Everyone is to think *sensibly*.

What does this mean? Simply put, it means we should not overestimate our value. We must not move with exaggerated self-esteem. Peter said,

> In the same way, you who are younger, be subject to the elders. All of you clothe yourselves with humility toward one another, because God resists the proud but gives grace to the humble. Humble yourselves, therefore, under the mighty hand of God, so that he may exalt you at the proper time, 1 Peter 5:5–6.

Sensibly

Thinking *sensibly* means to "be in your right mind." (Other translations use *sober judgment* here.) Don't think too high. Don't think too low. Don't underestimate yourself by saying you're *nothing* and any talent you have is minimal. Don't overestimate yourself and boast.

A lack of balance with self-perception can significantly damage God's church. Have a balanced estimate of yourself and the gifts you possess.

Humility

What is your understanding of humility? How do you define it? Write down some of your thoughts:

Did you start to write down "quiet," "invisible," or "out of the way?" Would these be accurate definitions? Why/why not?

Would you describe Peter or Paul in this way? Explain.

Look again at verse 3. Notice how Paul was not afraid to say he was an apostle by the grace of God. He was not afraid to say God had given him gifts of communicating the word. *Humility is not over-estimation or under-estimation—it is the right estimation.*

Moving Forward with Faith

The second part of Romans 12:3 transitions into what will be said in vv. 4–8. What talents do you have? Who gave them to you? *Whatever you have, you have because it is a gift from God to you.* God is calling on you to sharpen and refine these things, but the gifts you possess are His gifts to you. This makes your life a life of stewardship. You have been given a new life for His glory in the advancement of the kingdom.

Since God has given you gifts, they should not go unused. *God arranged the members in the body, each one of them, as He chose,* 1 Corinthians 12:18. God has given you your gifts because it pleases Him. He wants you to use it. Don't depreciate it. Don't second guess God because He gave it for the sake of His glory.

Conclusion

Reread Romans 12:1–3.

1. What is the motivation?

2. What is the mandate?

3. What is to be our attitude toward this world?

4. With what attitude are we to move forward as we live out the mandate?

5. How has this lesson challenged you personally?

Lesson 5

Where Do You Fit?

Romans 12:4–8

Introduction

Thus far in our lessons, we have discussed our spiritual motivation (Romans 12:1a). We talked about the mandate (Romans 12:1b). We reminded ourselves about our attitude toward the world and the need to be transformed (Romans 12:2). And we've seen the appeal in Romans 12:3 to fill our lives with humility, thinking sensibly.

Now, we will move forward to Paul's writing in Romans 12:4–8. Most of our Christian life is spent inside the realm of using our spiritual gifts and interacting with others. How do you manage the spiritual gifts God has blessed you with while working with other brothers and sisters in the body?

> Now as we have many parts in one body, and all the parts do not have the same function, in the same way we who are many are one body in Christ and individually members of one another. According to the grace given to us, we have different gifts: If prophecy, use it according to the proportion of one's faith; if service, use it in service; if teaching, in teaching; if exhorting, in exhortation; giving, with generosity; leading, with diligence; showing mercy, with cheerfulness (Romans 12:4–8).

Let us consider:

- Paul's illustration of the human body.
- The need for unity.
- Diversity is an asset, not a liability.

A Look at the Human Body

Let's look closely at 12:4–5. We each have many members in our physical body. Our body parts do not all have the same function or practice. We have one body, but many members are working together. Think of all the processes going on inside you. Many things are happening. Your heart and lungs are doing their work. Your immune system is aggressively attacking any threats. You rarely think about it.

This is what is to happen inside the church. We share our everyday lives, gifts, ministry, and resources. We have joy and sorrow every day. We share *everything*.

God has designed His spiritual body to work harmoniously like the body. What must you address for His body to function as He designed?

The Need for Unity

Now, let's examine 12:6–8. Notice how Paul emphasizes unity. We're all one, yet diverse. See how he encourages us to use our gifts proportionately *to our faith*. In other words, as God has measured, we use them. And, as we move forward, we encourage others to use their gifts.

Look with a positive view. Who is someone you can encourage *today?* How will you do this?

Which do you think humans tend to do more: Criticize? Or encourage? Why?

When you give in to criticizing someone, what is a typical motive? What is the cure for this?

How can you better appreciate your brothers and sisters uniqueness and the talents they bring to the family?

Appreciating Unity in Diversity

Did that heading cause a particular reaction in your mind? If you're like me, you are probably skeptical of it because it is so abused in the religious world. But, the general concept of unity in diversity is biblical. It's viewed in a very positive way right here in our text. Diversity within a congregation should be viewed as an asset. Think of it this way. Diversity is what makes your body work. It is the same principle in the church. If one part doesn't work, the entire body suffers. God did not make one of us the same.

Our diversity in gifts, talents, race, and life experiences within the local church family is not a liability—it's an opportunity! Each of us has a unique, special place in the body. We should embrace that and use it for everything God intends.

Conclusion

1. What ties our life, gifts, ministry, and resources together? Does this knowledge affect your viewpoint on unity?

2. How do everyday joys and sorrows bring us together?

3. How has the world abused the Biblical concept of *unity in diversity?* How can we respond to this error?

4. What are some things you can do to better appreciate the diversity within your church family?

Lesson 6

Genuine Love

Romans 12:9

Introduction

Motivated by the mercy of God, we surrender as a living sacrifice for service to God. Each of us is in the process of transformation, reorienting our thinking from an earthly worldview to the spiritual. These things do not happen inside a vacuum, however. There are many others alongside us, and as we work together inside God's family, we must maintain a proper attitude toward who we are and appreciate others for who they are. Romans 12:4–8 is a call to respect the unity in diversity found within the body of Christ.

As we begin to survey the next section of the chapter, verses 9–21 encourage us to maintain the unity God has blessed us with. All the principles in this section are continuous and stressed in the present tense. These things should be a continuing quality of our lives.

This lesson will focus on Romans 12:9 …

> Let love be without hypocrisy. Detest evil; cling to what is good.

Let's learn about:

- Paul's call for genuine love.
- The warning to hate evil.
- Cling to what is good.

Love with a Genuine Love

Love should characterize the Christian. It is the essence of the law, Matthew 22:36–40. The foundation is love in the conduct of God's son or daughter, inside and outside the church. It finds itself at the center of Paul's teaching. It is the first in several lists Paul used on practical Christian principles for everyday life. See Galatians 5:22–23 and 1 Corinthians 13:1–13.

Notice Paul's admonition in Romans 12:9. *Let love be genuine.* The original word means "without a mask." This means that Christians are to love in an "unhypocritical, unfeigned way." It is love without pretense or slander. Positively speaking, it is the type of love that is consistent and sincere. Two things demonstrate it:

- A selfless attitude.
- Selfless giving.

This love is not so much about emotion or sentimentality as it is about the needs of others. It's the type of love Jesus called for.

> "I give you a new command: Love one another. Just as I have loved you, you are also to love one another. By this everyone will know that you are my disciples, if you love one another" (John 13:34–35).

It has been said there is no vice worse than hypocrisy. Just as there is no virtue surpassing love, hypocritical love is the ultimate moral contradiction.

Be prepared to discuss the significant damage that can arise from insincere love. How does it affect relationships in your family and the church?

What are some ways we can love genuinely? (What does selfless love look like?)

Hate What is Evil

Since Romans 12:9a is to be understood as an imperative, *let love be genuine*, the natural question is how? How can we accomplish selfless giving? The answer is explained in the following sentence in the verse through 12:21, but we want to train our focus on Romans 12:9b and 12:9c for this lesson.

Hate and *cling* are very forceful words. *Hate* expresses a strong feeling of horror. Words like "abhorrence, disgust, and loathing" are associated with it. *Cling* means to attach yourself closely to something. It carries with it the idea of never letting go. There is nothing passive about either word. Evil and hatred are very general terms. They encompass everything morally wicked and ungodly.

Cling to What is Good

A person who loves will move with enthusiasm, demonstrating a solid loathing for all that is evil. Rather than holding to what is evil, Christians must glue themselves to what is good. Again, see the action implied in the word's usage. This is not speaking of casual approval of good things; instead, it is the commitment to the way of goodness. It means our whole life is to be wrapped up in it. This type of good involves the right attitude and positive deeds.

Read through the following passages and write down the words that indicate what our attitude should be:

Romans 13:12–14:

1 Corinthians 13:6:

Colossians 3:8:

1 Thessalonians 5:21–22:

1 Peter 2:1:

Conclusion

Today, many believers have a general tolerance for deviant behavior. **Evil is the enemy of all that leads to Christ.**

1. How can you relate *clinging to what is good* back to the principle of selfless love talked about earlier in the verse? Explain.

2. What are some of the influences that might persuade us to lessen our grip on what is good?

3. How can this affect the relationships we have inside the church?

Lesson 7

Outdo One Another in Showing Honor

Romans 12:10

Introduction

Romans 12:9–21 contains a set of appeals to explain how we maintain the unity God has blessed us with. Every principle in this section is continuous and stressed in the present tense. In other words, they should be a continuing quality of our lives.

In the previous lesson, we focused on *genuine love*. This type of love expresses itself in sincerity and without pretense. It is not so much about emotion or sentimentality as about the needs of others.

Now, we will examine Romans 12:10:

> Love one another deeply as brothers and sisters. Take the lead in honoring one another.

Let's consider:

- The need for deep love.
- What it means to show honor to one another.

Deep Love

The wording in the first part of 12:10 is essential. In this verse, *love* is a compound word (*philostorgoi*) that denotes "tender affection among family, especially the mutual love of parents and children." This is the only place in the New Testament where the word is used. The NIV translates the word as "devoted." It emphasizes blood ties and the type of attachment sealed by nature. Of course, Paul implies that we make the application to how we love our brothers and sisters in Christ.

Relationships among Christians should involve familiarity, understanding, and acceptance. We should consider the local church as our immediate family and the church universally as our extended family. Fellow Christians are due the appropriate affection and devotion among brothers and sisters.

What It Means to Show Honor to One Another

Membership inside the local body is about something other than personal status. The idea presented in our text stresses the need to go out of our way to esteem others. Take a moment to reread Romans 12:4–8. While some of the spiritual gifts mentioned in this passage are no longer around, think of the general meaning of the passage.

Different people have been blessed with various talents of differing types and measures. But, no matter who you are in the body, you can exhibit your talent of honoring others. This is one of the most powerful personal ministries we have. Today, we live in an age of individual achievement where many people feel unappreciated. Every day, you can demonstrate appreciation for the deeds of others. This is the fulfillment of passages like:

- And let us consider one another to provoke love and good works, (Hebrews 10:24).
- Rejoice with those who rejoice; weep with those who weep, (Romans 12:15).
- Do nothing out of selfish ambition or conceit, but in humility consider others as more important than yourselves. Everyone should look not to his own interests, but rather to the interests of others (Philippians 2:3–4).
- Therefore encourage one another and build each other up as you are already doing (1 Thessalonians 5:11).
- Instruct them to do what is good, to be rich in good works, to be generous and willing to share (1 Timothy 6:18).
- I am not saying this as a command. Rather, by means of the diligence of others, I am testing the genuineness of your love, (2 Corinthians 8:8).

Conclusion

1. Besides Romans 12:10, can you think of other passages that identify the necessity of a loving relationship between brethren?

2. What is significant about the word *love* in 12:10? What does it mean in the original language?

3. How does this apply to the way we live inside the church?

4. What is the key to developing this type of love with brethren? How strong are your relationships with your brothers and sisters outside the church building?

5. What are some things that keep you from knowing your brethren better?

6. Who is someone in your church family you do not know well? Write down a few names. What can *you do* to strengthen the relationship you have with them? *What will you do this week to do so?*

7. What is the idea behind Romans 12:10b? What are some ways you can improve in this?

Lesson 8

Fervent in the Spirit

Romans 12:11

Introduction

Previously, we focused on *showing each other honor*. We move with *deep love* or brotherly affection. Fellow Christians are due affection and devotion that is proper among saints. We discussed how membership inside the local body is about something other than personal status. We need to go out of our way to esteem others highly.

This lesson focuses on Romans 12:11, where Paul says,

> Do not lack diligence in zeal; be fervent in the Spirit; serve the Lord.

It is also interesting to consider how this verse is presented in the NIV: *Never be lacking in zeal, but keep your spiritual fervor, serving the Lord.* This verse is a collection of three short imperatives in the original language.

- Do not lack diligence in zeal.
- Be fervent in spirit.
- Serve the Lord.

Let's examine each of these sentences in detail.

Do Not Lack Diligence in Zeal

The ESV uses the term *slothful* here. What picture comes to your mind when you think of that word? It presents a particular image. The idea is that we need to be confident, active, and complacent. This hesitation may come from general weariness, fear, bashfulness, or reserve. Humans are prone to ups and downs. This is especially true in the spiritual realm. The world and its forces come at us hard. This is why we see constant admonition to endure and push through. Consider the teaching of these parallel passages:

- As for you, brothers, do not grow weary in doing good, (2 Thessalonians 3:13).
- For God gave us a spirit not of fear but of power and love and self-control (2 Timothy 1:7).
- Since then we have a great high priest who has passed through the heavens, Jesus, the Son of God, let us hold fast our confession, (Hebrews 4:14).
- Blessed is the man who remains steadfast under trial, for when he has stood the test he will receive the crown of life, which God has promised to those who love him, (James 1:12).
- Here is a call for the endurance of the saints, those who keep the commandments of God and their faith in Jesus (Revelation 14:12).
- "The one who conquers will have this heritage, and I will be his God and he will be my son. But as for the cowardly, the faithless, the detestable, as for murderers, the sexually immoral, sorcerers, idolaters, and all liars, their portion will be in the lake that burns with fire and sulfur, which is the second death," (Revelation 21:7–8).

But besides focusing only on a weary spirit, sometimes a lack of diligence carries a rebellious connotation. It speaks about an attitude that tries to get by with as little work and inconvenience as possible. This disposition shrinks from dust and heat and resents the necessity for any exertion as a burden and imposition. Those who possess such attitudes should be admonished.

Fervent in Zeal

In this context, *zeal* refers to "haste" or "rapidity." Simply put, the matters of the Christian life demand haste. Everything has urgency.

Do. It. Now.

Fervent comes from the Greek *zeo*, meaning "to bubble, boil, seethe, or burn." It often refers to water boiling or metal glowing with heat. In scripture, it is frequently used metaphorically, speaking of being full of energy or being on fire with zeal and enthusiasm. The Christian life cannot be dull. If it is, something is not right. Moving with enthusiasm means that we possess eagerness, passion, and confidence.

The appeal here is that we are glowing or burning with the Spirit. Each of us is to allow ourselves to be set afire by the Holy Spirit. This fire is not kindled through externals but rather the inner part of us energized by God's word.

How fired up are you for Christian service?

Serve the Lord

Here, *the Lord* refers to Jesus. He is our master. We are His servants. Our service involves external obedience and an inner spiritual attitude of submission to His authority over us. He rules our heart, Colossians 3:15–17. Paul called for obedience from the heart in Romans 6:17. This attitude involves the acceptance of our new reality. Reading the immediate context around that verse demonstrates that we are to present ourselves as *slaves* to God. See Romans 6:16, 18, 22.

Our obedience to the gospel brings a responsibility to adhere to God's expectations. Are you disciplining your body? See 1 Corinthians 9:27.

Conclusion

1. What image comes to your mind when you think of the word *slothful*? Explain.

2. What things have come up in your life that have led to hesitation, fear, or reserve in following through with your spiritual needs? How did you overcome it? Who gets the credit? Why?

3. In what ways could *slothfulness* equal rebellion? Explain.

4. Why are spiritual matters to be addressed with a *do–it–now* urgency?

5. *The Christian life cannot be dull.* Do you agree with this statement? Explain.

6. How do we allow ourselves to be "set on fire" by the Spirit?

7. What does it mean to obey God from the heart?

8. What connotation is associated with the words *serve* and *slave?* How does this apply to our spiritual service?

9. What are some things you can do this week to increase your spiritual hunger?

Lesson 9

Rejoice in Hope

Romans 12:12

Introduction

Previously, we focused on being *fervent in spirit*. The Christian life is not to be dull. Instead, our spiritual life is to be set on fire by the Spirit, where we are constantly moving with a sense of urgency to do the things of God. We understand this is part of our responsibility as servants of our Lord Jesus Christ.

This lesson looks at Romans 12:12:

> Rejoice in hope, be patient in tribulation, be constant in prayer.

Like the previous verse, this verse is a collection of three short imperatives in the original language.

- Rejoice in hope.
- Be patient in tribulation.
- Be constant in prayer.

Let's study each of these sentences in detail.

Rejoice in Hope

The New Testament continually encourages us to rejoice in hope. No matter what happens on earth, we are to *rejoice and be glad, for your reward is great in heaven, for so they persecuted the prophets who were before you,* Matthew 5:12. Paul spoke a great deal about the need to rejoice. Read Philippians 3:1 and 4:4. In Revelation 19:6–7, victory and rejoicing are seen after the great victory over evil.

What is the source of our joy? Hope. This is all based on the grace bestowed in Jesus. Hope is nothing more than a confident expectation of salvation. The idea is that no matter our present circumstances, we can be joyful when we think of our future reward. It is living and dynamic, 1 Peter 1:3–4. We approach this with the eagerness of a pilgrim going home.

Be Patient in Tribulation

Hope is inspired by joy and gives us the courage to bear up under present afflictions. What might these afflictions be?

- They could be physical suffering, sickness, disease, etc.
- They could be spiritual or physical persecution.

There are many warnings and exhortations in scripture to be faithful during difficult times.

- "I have told you these things so that in me you may have peace. You will have suffering in this world. Be courageous! I have conquered the world" (John 16:33).
- Through many hardships to enter the kingdom of God (Acts 14:22).
- I said to him, "Sir, you know." Then he told me: These are the ones coming out of the great tribulation. They washed their robes and made them white in the blood of the Lamb (Revelation 7:14).

Patient may not be the best translated word. In the original language, the word is closer to the meaning of "holding out steadfastly." It is the ability to bear up under whatever comes, carrying the idea of courage with it.

Be Constant in Prayer

During times of difficulty, it might be easy for us to shrink back in our prayer life. However, we must resist that tendency and move with constant diligence in engaging God in prayer. "Constant" refers to the type of effort that never lets up. Also, the concept of confident expectation for an answer or results is involved here. Think of what the scriptures teach regarding our prayer life:

- Luke 18:1—pray with persistence.
- Ephesians 6:18—pray at all times.
- 1 Thessalonians 5:17—pray without ceasing.

Prayer should be a significant aspect of a Christian's life.

Conclusion

1. What are some spiritual things in which you can rejoice? List at least three things below.

2. What is the source of our rejoicing?

3. How would you define your spiritual hope? What attitude(s) are involved in it?

4. In what ways is the world pressing in on you? How are you presently exhibiting patience? Explain.

5. How does one grow in courage?

6. Why is persistent prayer so essential for the Christian?

7. Who are some individuals you can pray for specifically this week?

8. How might this help them if you let them know you're praying for them? How will it help you?

9. If you're not praying like you should, what are some things you will do this week to do it more?

Lesson 10

Contributing to the Needs of the Saints

Romans 12:13

Introduction

In Romans 12:9–21, we find a more concise collection of ethical injunctions nowhere else in Paul's writings. They are each basic to practical Christian living.

Previously, we focused on what it means to rejoice in hope. We then examined the other two sentences in the lesson, which focus on being patient in tribulation and constant in prayer.

Now, we will think on Romans 12:13:

> Contribute to the needs of the saints and seek to show hospitality.

Like the previous verses, Romans 12.13 is a collection of short imperatives. Here we find two:

- Contribute to the needs of the saints.
- Seek to show hospitality.

Let's look at both sentences in detail.

Contribute to the Needs of the Saints

Both sentences in 12:13 fall under the general heading of benevolence. Christians need to cultivate the spirit of giving. I like how the NIV translates the first sentence of the verse: *share with God's people who are in need*. What, exactly, are the needs of the saints?

Sharing could refer to physical needs such as food and clothing. It refers "to fellowship, sharing, and participation in." Sometimes, sharing refers to a gift of money or material goods to provide for the needs of the poor or gospel preachers.

However, this is more than just covering the outward act of giving. It goes further. Christians must be willing to identify themselves with the needs of others *and make them their own.* In other words, our giving should be from the heart. Moses Lard once wrote, "When the children of God fall into want, take a part of their wants upon yourselves. Make their wants your wants to the full extent of your ability to relieve them."

The bottom line is that every Christian is responsible for participating in the church's ministry of benevolence to some degree. See Galatians 6:10.

Seek to Show Hospitality

Hospitality is literally "the love of strangers." It is the act of treating a stranger as a friend. This would have had an obvious meaning for the first–century Christians, especially assisting those who traveled. During these times, it was tough to find safe and affordable accommodations. "In most ancient cultures, hospitality was a prized virtue." It is also seen throughout the New Testament as a critical fundamental of everyday Christian practice:

- " For I was hungry and you gave me something to eat; I was thirsty and you gave me something to drink; I was a stranger and you took me in, (Matthew 25:35).
- Don't neglect to show hospitality, for by doing this some have welcomed angels as guests without knowing it, (Hebrews 13:2).
- Be hospitable to one another without complaining (1 Peter 4:9).
- Dear friend, you are faithful in whatever you do for the brothers and sisters, especially when they are strangers. They have testified to your love before the church. You will do well to send them on their journey in a manner worthy of God since they set out for the sake of the Name, accepting nothing from pagans. Therefore, we ought to support such people as coworkers of the truth (3 John 5–8).

Show, as used in Romans 12:13b, is a powerful verb. It means to "run after, to chase, to pursue, to strive for, to aspire, or seek after earnestly." It must be taken seriously and is a priority for the Christian.

Conclusion

1. Why is the spirit of giving such an important Christian principle?

2. What are some examples of how we share with others?

3. Is there more to this than simple financial or physical assistance? i.e., what type of heart are we to have as we give?

4. Is there anyone you know of who needs help? How can you help?

5. What does it mean to be hospitable?

6. What should be our attitude toward hospitality?

7. What keeps us from practicing hospitality as much as we should?

8. What are some things you can do to be more hospitable?

Lesson 11

Bless Those Who Persecute You

Romans 12:14

Introduction

Previously, we focused on contributing to the needs of the saints. Christians need to cultivate the spirit of giving, even to the level of feeling the needs of others. Every Christian is responsible for participating in the church's ministry of benevolence to some degree. See Galatians 6:10. This principle is also illustrated in hospitality, "the love of strangers." We should make these matters a priority.

This lesson focuses on Romans 12:14 where Paul says, "Bless those who persecute you; bless and do not curse."

Let's explore this verse in detail.

Christians Expect Persecution

Jesus did not speak of persecution in theoretical terms but in reality. He promised it would come:

- Blessed are those who are persecuted because of righteousness, for the kingdom of heaven is theirs. "You are blessed when they insult you and persecute you and falsely say every kind of evil against you because of me, (Matthew 5:10–11).
- Remember the word I spoke to you: 'A servant is not greater than his master.' If they persecuted me, they will also persecute you. If they kept my word, they will also keep yours, (John 15:20).

Paul also confirmed this in 2 Timothy 3:12: *In fact, all who want to live a godly life in Christ Jesus will be persecuted.*

Our passage in focus for this lesson carries two principles:

- We must endure persecution.
- We must refrain from striking back.

We Must Endure Persecution

When it comes, we must push through. Think of these companion passages:

- Dear friends, don't be surprised when the fiery ordeal comes among you to test you, as if something unusual were happening to you. Instead, rejoice as you share in the sufferings of Christ so that you may also rejoice with great joy when his glory is revealed (1 Peter 4:12–13).
- Don't be afraid of what you are about to suffer. Look, the devil is about to throw some of you into prison to test you, and you will experience affliction for ten days. Be faithful to the point of death, and I will give you the crown of life, (Revelation 2:10).
- Now I want you to know, brothers and sisters, that what has happened to me has actually advanced the gospel, so that it has become known throughout the whole imperial guard, and to everyone else, that my imprisonment is because I am in Christ. Most of the brothers have gained confidence in the Lord from my imprisonment and dare even more to speak the word fearlessly (Philippians 1:12–14).

We Must Refrain from Striking Back

This is utterly contrary to human nature. Notice the second part of our verse: *bless and do not curse*, Romans 12:14b. This requires a powerful act of will, and the need to handle our persecutors in this fashion is repeated throughout the scriptures.

This is why we must be committed to *renewing our minds (12:2) and living inside the transformed life.* We must move forward in solid trust in God's promises. Some things may not be possible on a human level, but they become possible with God's help.

Please think of the example we have to draw from in scripture. For example, Jesus was successful in holding back:

- Then Jesus said, "Father, forgive them, because they do not know what they are doing." And they divided his clothes and cast lots, (Luke 23:34).
- For you were called to this, because Christ also suffered for you, leaving you an example, that you should follow in his steps. He did not commit sin, and no deceit was found in his mouth; when he was insulted, he did not insult in return; when he suffered, he did not threaten but entrusted

himself to the one who judges justly (1 Peter 2:21–23).
- He knelt down and cried out with a loud voice, "Lord, do not hold this sin against them!" And after saying this, he fell asleep (Acts 7:60).

This is all according to Jesus's commands:

- But I tell you, love your enemies and pray for those who persecute you (Matthew 5:44).
- Bless those who curse you, pray for those who mistreat you, (Luke 6:28).

Conclusion

1. How did Jesus refer to persecution? How did Paul? (Will it come?)

2. How do you define Christian *persecution*?

3. What kind of "persecution" have Americans experienced throughout the nation's existence? Speculate what type of "persecutions" could be coming in the future. Why?

4. How can you prepare for any future "persecutions?"

5. When persecution comes, what must we do? (12.14b)

6. How is this possible?

7. What type of example did Jesus set as He handled all sorts of persecution?

8. How can Stephen's example inspire you?

9. How does all this fit back into the teaching of 12.1–2?

Lesson 12

Live in Harmony with One Another

Romans 12:16–21

Introduction

Over the last six lessons, we have discussed various appeals that are continuing qualities of our lives. Each one of them is fundamental to christian living. Previously, we focused on the need to bless those who persecute us. Persecution is a fact associated with christian life, as shown in Matthew 5:10–11, John 15:20, and 2 Timothy 3:12. We have been called to endure it and refrain from striking back, even blessing those who strike out against us. Jesus and Stephen serve as excellent examples of how to find victory.

This lesson examines Romans 12:16–21:

> Live in harmony with one another. Do not be proud; instead, associate with the humble. Do not be wise in your own estimation. Do not repay anyone evil for evil. Give careful thought to do what is honorable in everyone's eyes. If possible, as far as it depends on you, live at peace with everyone. Friends, do not avenge yourselves; instead, leave room for God's wrath, because it is written, Vengeance belongs to me; I will repay, says the Lord. But if your enemy is hungry, feed him. If he is thirsty, give him something to drink. For in so doing you will be heaping fiery coals on his head. Do not be conquered by evil, but conquer evil with good.

We'll discuss the following principles:

- Live in harmony with each other.
- Do what is honorable in the sight of all.
- Live peacefully with everyone.

Live in Harmony with Each Other

How can we fulfill this expectation? We must rid ourselves of pride. Pride often results in discord between brethren. It drives people to think they need preferential treatment. Most cases of personal conflict, from the largest to the most minor, result from someone who thinks they are better than someone else or has done something to us.

So, the directive is to *live in harmony with one another,* 12:16. This is less about accommodating someone than about arriving at a mental understanding and adoption of God's way of thinking. The more we surrender ourselves and align our hearts with God, the closer we will be to each other.

Pride destroys the harmony of the body. So, Paul says *not to be haughty but to associate with the lowly.* The warning here is to purposely adjust ourselves to humble situations and take a genuine interest in ordinary people. Think of how 12:16b is an application of what we have studied thus far:

- demonstrate sincere love, 12:9a
- show mutual honor and respect, 12:10b
- participate in gifts of sharing, 12:13
- practice empathetic joy or sorrow, 12:15

There are humble tasks and ordinary people who need our attention. We are not above any other person in the kingdom. We need to look at all people in the same way.

Next, Paul says, *never be wise in your own sight.* No person is ever to assume he or she has complete knowledge. Admonitions against this type of mindset are seen throughout scripture. Here are two examples from the Old Testament:

Woe to those who consider themselves wise and judge themselves clever (Isaiah 5:21).

Don't be wise in your own eyes; fear the LORD and turn away from evil (Proverbs 3:7).

Do What is Honorable in the Sight of All

Why are many tempted to take revenge? It may often come down to an exalted view of oneself. Each one of us lives on our own stage. But we are called not to repay anyone evil for evil but to give careful thought to doing what is honorable in everyone's eyes (Romans 12:17).

Everyone is watching. How will we respond to mistreatment? Will we:

- Turn the other cheek, Matthew 5:39
- Go the second mile, Matthew 5:41
- Do good to all, Galatians 6:10, always seeking to do good, 1 Thessalonians 5:15?
- Bless, so that we may obtain a blessing, 1 Peter 3:9?

In olden times, Solomon said, *never let loyalty and faithfulness leave you. Tie them around your neck; write them on the tablet of your heart. Then you will find favor and high regard with God and people* (Proverbs 3:3–4).

Live Peacefully with Everyone

Romans 12:18 is a passage that hits many of us squarely in the face. While it is not possible in every case to have peace, this passage does place the element of personal responsibility on us to do what it takes to live in peace. *So far as it depends on you.* This type of disposition is driven by genuine trust in God. We know that everything is in God's hands. If there is mistreatment by others, we trust He will right the wrong. Thus, we find what Paul says next in 12:19–21:

> Friends, do not avenge yourselves; instead, leave room for God's wrath, because it is written, Vengeance belongs to me; I will repay, says the Lord. But If your enemy is hungry, feed him. If he is thirsty, give him something to drink. For in so doing you will be heaping fiery coals on his head. Do not be conquered by evil, but conquer evil with good.

We are never to take vengeance into our hands. The person close to God understands and trusts He will deal with it in His way in His own time. Paul certainly lived with this perspective: *since it is just for God to repay those who afflict you* (2 Thessalonians 1:6). Christians have been called upon to refrain from helping God carry out His divine retribution.

Rather than take revenge, we are to feed our enemy when he or she is hungry. We are to give them something to drink when they are thirsty. What is the intended result? Doing so will make them feel a burning sense of shame.

Remember, right always prevails against wrong. God is always on His throne. God is in control.

Conclusion

1. How does pride create discord in the body?

2. What does it mean to *live in harmony with one another?*

3. Why is it important to remember that every person is on an equal playing field in the kingdom?

4. Why is it so deadly to interpersonal relationships to think of ourselves as higher than someone else?

5. Why is it so important to conduct ourselves in honor?

6. How much effort will this require? Will it require forethought? How can we prepare to do the honorable thing before the persecution/problem comes?

7. Think of times you have been mistreated and responded in kind. What attitude(s) led to your failure to live by the expectations listed in today's reading? Be prepared to discuss.

8. What is our responsibility toward peace?

9. What enables a person not to retaliate when mistreated?

10. How can you strengthen your trust in God so that you can live out 12:19–21?

www.ingramcontent.com/pod-product-compliance
Lightning Source LLC
Chambersburg PA
CBHW042350040426
42449CB00018B/3478